# The Ultimate Guide to Real Estate Broker Licenses in All 50 States and D.C.

ROBERTO MIGUEL RODRIGUEZ

Copyright Page

TITLE: The Ultimate Guide to Real Estate Broker Licenses in All 50 States and D.C.

1<sup>ST</sup> Edition



ISBN: 9798223900818

# Table of Contents

The Ultimate Guide to Real Estate Broker Licenses in all 50 States and D.C.: A Step-by-Step Approach for Real Estate Agents

By Roberto Miguel Rodriguez

# Chapter 1: Introduction to Real Estate Broker Licenses

Understanding the Importance of a Real Estate Broker License

In the world of real estate, obtaining a broker license is an essential step for both real estate agents and the public. A real estate broker license provides individuals with the legal authority to represent clients in real estate transactions, offering a higher level of expertise and professionalism. This subchapter aims to shed light on the significance of a real estate broker license and its benefits for real estate agents and the public.

For real estate agents, obtaining a broker license is a natural progression in their career. It signifies a higher level of expertise and knowledge in the field, allowing agents to take on more responsibilities and expand their business. With a broker license, agents can supervise other real estate agents, open their own brokerage firm, and even hire and train new agents. This level of autonomy and leadership can lead to increased earning potential and career advancement.

Moreover, a real estate broker license provides agents with a competitive edge in the industry. Clients are more likely to trust and choose a licensed broker over an agent without a license, as it demonstrates a commitment to professionalism and ethical standards. It also allows brokers to access a wider range of properties and listings, expanding their network and client base.

For the public, working with a licensed real estate broker offers numerous advantages. Brokers undergo rigorous training and education, ensuring a deep understanding of the complexities of the real estate market. They possess the necessary skills to navigate legal and financial aspects of transactions, protecting their clients' interests and mitigating risks. A licensed broker also has access to a broader network of industry professionals, such as lenders, appraisers, and inspectors, further streamlining the buying or selling process.

Furthermore, a broker license provides an added layer of accountability and consumer protection. Licensed brokers are bound by strict codes of conduct and ethical guidelines, ensuring that clients receive fair and transparent representation. In the event of any disputes or issues, clients have access to grievance procedures and can seek recourse through regulatory bodies.

In conclusion, understanding the importance of a real estate broker license is crucial for both real estate agents and the public. It offers agents career advancement opportunities, increased earning potential, and a competitive edge. For the public, working with a licensed broker provides expertise, professionalism, and consumer protection. Whether you are a real estate agent looking to take your career to the next level or a prospective buyer or seller seeking trustworthy representation, obtaining a real estate broker license is an essential step in the process.

How a Real Estate Broker License Can Benefit Your Career

Obtaining a real estate broker license can be a game-changer for your career in the real estate industry. Whether you are a real estate agent looking to take your career to the next level or someone considering a career change, a broker license can open up a world of opportunities and benefits.

First and foremost, a real estate broker license gives you credibility and a professional edge. As a licensed broker, you have undergone extensive training and education, which sets you apart from the competition. Clients are more likely to trust and seek the services of a licensed broker, knowing that you have the knowledge and expertise to guide them through complex real estate transactions.

Furthermore, a broker license allows you to operate your own real estate brokerage firm. This means you have the freedom to build your own brand, set your own business goals, and establish your own team of agents. Running your own brokerage gives you the opportunity to increase your income potential and have more control over your professional destiny.

In addition, having a broker license opens up a wider range of professional opportunities. Many states have specific requirements for certain real estate activities, such as property management or commercial real estate transactions. With a broker license, you can expand your services and specialize in these areas, attracting a larger client base and increasing your earning potential.

A real estate broker license also provides you with the opportunity to mentor and train new agents. As a broker, you have the ability to hire and supervise agents, sharing your knowledge and expertise to help them succeed in their careers. This not only benefits your brokerage but also allows you to make a positive impact on the next generation of real estate professionals.

Lastly, a broker license can open doors for professional networking and advancement. Real estate industry associations and organizations often prioritize licensed brokers for leadership positions and committee roles. By actively participating in these groups, you can expand your network, stay updated on industry trends, and position yourself as a trusted expert in the field.

In conclusion, obtaining a real estate broker license can greatly benefit your career. From increased credibility and professional opportunities to the potential for higher income and personal growth, a broker license is a worthwhile investment in your future. Whether you are a real estate agent or someone interested in entering the industry, taking the steps to become a licensed broker will undoubtedly propel your career forward.

Exploring the Different Types of Real Estate Licenses

In the vast and ever-changing world of real estate, there are various types of licenses that professionals can obtain to practice legally in their respective states. Understanding the different types of real estate licenses is crucial for both real estate agents and the public. In this subchapter, we will delve into the intricacies of these licenses and shed light on their significance in different states across the United States.

One of the most comprehensive and informative real estate license guides available, "The Ultimate Guide to Real Estate Broker Licenses in All 50 States and D.C.: A Step-by-Step Approach for Real Estate Agents and the Public," aims to provide an in-depth understanding of the licensing process in each state and the District of Columbia.

Whether you aspire to become a licensed real estate broker in California, Texas, New York, Florida, Illinois, Pennsylvania, Georgia, Ohio, Virginia, Washington, D.C., or any other state, this guide is an invaluable resource. It offers a step-by-step approach and covers the specific requirements and application processes for each state, ensuring that aspiring brokers are well-equipped to navigate the licensing process successfully.

This subchapter will serve as a comprehensive overview of the various types of real estate licenses, highlighting the key differences and similarities between states. It will explore the different classifications of licenses, such as salesperson licenses, broker licenses, associate broker licenses, and managing broker licenses. Furthermore, it will provide insights into the educational requirements, examination procedures, experience prerequisites, and continuing education requirements associated with each license type.

By delving into the nuances of real estate licensing, this subchapter aims to empower real estate agents and the public with the knowledge and understanding necessary to make informed decisions about their real estate careers and transactions. Whether you are a seasoned professional or just starting in the industry, this subchapter will prove to be an invaluable resource on your journey to obtaining a real estate broker license.

"The Ultimate Guide to Real Estate Broker Licenses in All 50 States and D.C." is a comprehensive and user-friendly resource that caters to the needs of real estate agents and the public alike. By exploring the different types of real estate licenses, readers will gain a deeper understanding of the licensing process and the requirements associated with each state. With this knowledge at hand, individuals can confidently pursue their real estate goals and make informed decisions about their careers and investments.

Overview of the Licensing Process in All 50 States and D.C.

Obtaining a real estate broker license can be a daunting task, especially when each state has its own unique requirements and processes. This subchapter aims to provide an overview of the licensing process in all 50 states and D.C., catering to real estate agents, the public, and various niches interested in specific state licensing guidelines.

The licensing process, regardless of the state, typically involves completing educational requirements, passing an exam, submitting an application, and meeting additional state-specific requirements. However, the specific details and requirements can vary significantly from state to state.

For example, California is known for its stringent licensing process. Aspiring brokers in California must complete college-level real estate courses, accumulate experience as a licensed salesperson, and pass the state exam. On the other hand, Texas has a more streamlined process, requiring education, experience, and passing the state exam.

New York, Florida, Illinois, Pennsylvania, Georgia, Ohio, Virginia, and Washington, D.C. all have their own unique licensing requirements and processes, which will be discussed in detail in subsequent subchapters.

Understanding the licensing process is crucial for anyone considering a career as a real estate broker. It is important to be aware of the educational requirements, such as the number of pre-licensing courses or specific topics that need to be covered. Additionally, knowing the experience requirements, if any, and the duration of the licensing process is essential for planning and setting realistic expectations.

This subchapter will provide a comprehensive overview of each state's licensing process, covering the necessary steps from start to finish. It will detail the educational requirements, exam information, application procedures, and any additional requirements unique to each state.

Whether you are an aspiring real estate broker, a current agent looking to expand your capabilities, or a member of the public interested in understanding the licensing process, this subchapter will serve as a valuable resource. It will guide you through the steps needed to obtain a real estate broker license in each state, including the District of Columbia. With this knowledge, you can confidently navigate the complex world of real estate licensing and take the necessary steps to achieve your goals.

# Chapter 2: How to Get a Real Estate Broker License in California

Overview of the California Real Estate Broker License Requirements

Obtaining a real estate broker license in California is an important step for those looking to establish a thriving career in the real estate industry. The California Bureau of Real Estate (CalBRE) has set forth specific requirements and criteria that must be met in order to obtain this license. This chapter will provide an overview of the California real estate broker license requirements, outlining the necessary steps for aspiring brokers.

To become a licensed real estate broker in California, individuals must first meet certain eligibility criteria. These include being at least 18 years old, possessing a high school diploma or equivalent, and completing a minimum of two years of real estate salesperson experience within the last five years.

The next step entails completing the required coursework. California requires applicants to complete a total of eight college-level courses, covering various aspects of real estate such as real estate principles, real estate practice, legal aspects of real estate, and real estate finance. These courses can be taken at any accredited college or university, or through approved real estate schools.

After completing the required coursework, applicants must pass the California Real Estate Broker Examination. This exam assesses the knowledge and understanding of real estate laws, regulations, and practices in California. It is administered by the California Department of Real Estate (DRE) and consists of both a national and state-specific portion.

Once the examination is successfully passed, applicants must submit an application to the CalBRE, along with the required fees and supporting documents. These documents typically include proof of completion of the required coursework, proof of real estate experience, and fingerprints for a background check.

Additionally, applicants must obtain a California Bureau of Real Estate (CalBRE) sponsorship from a licensed real estate broker who will act as their employing broker. This sponsorship is necessary for the issuance of the broker license.

Upon meeting all the requirements and submitting a complete application, applicants will be notified of their eligibility for the real estate broker license. If approved, the license will be issued, allowing individuals to conduct real estate transactions in California as a licensed broker.

In conclusion, obtaining a real estate broker license in California requires individuals to meet specific eligibility requirements, complete the required coursework, pass the California Real Estate Broker Examination, and submit an application to the CalBRE. By following these steps, aspiring brokers can navigate the process and achieve their goal of becoming a licensed real estate broker in California.

Step-by-Step Guide to Obtaining a Real Estate Broker License in California

If you're looking to take your real estate career to the next level and become a licensed broker in California, this step-by-step guide will walk you through the process. Whether you're a real estate agent or a member of the public interested in pursuing a broker license, these steps will help you navigate the requirements and application process.

1. Meet the eligibility criteria: To become a licensed broker in California, you must be at least 18 years old, have a high school diploma or

equivalent, and complete a minimum of two years of real estate experience as a licensed salesperson or equivalent.

2. Complete the required coursework: California requires you to complete 8 college-level courses in various real estate topics. These courses cover subjects like real estate principles, real estate practice, and legal aspects of real estate. Make sure to choose an approved educational provider and complete the required coursework.

3. Gather the necessary documentation: Before applying for a broker license, you'll need to gather certain documents, including proof of completion of the required coursework, proof of legal presence in the United States, and proof of experience as a licensed salesperson.

4. Submit your application: Once you have completed the coursework and gathered the necessary documents, you can submit your application for a broker license to the California Department of Real Estate (DRE). Pay the required application fee and await further instructions from the DRE.

5. Pass the state exam: After your application is processed, the DRE will provide you with an examination schedule. You'll need to pass the state exam, which consists of both a national and state-specific portion, to obtain your broker license.

6. Complete the fingerprinting process: As part of the application process, you'll be required to complete a Live Scan fingerprinting process. This is to ensure that you meet the necessary background check requirements.

7. Activate your license: Once you have successfully passed the state exam and completed the fingerprinting process, you can activate your broker license. You will need to pay the necessary fees and provide proof of errors and omissions insurance.

By following these step-by-step instructions, you can obtain your real estate broker license in California. Whether you're a real estate agent looking to advance your career or a member of the public interested in becoming a licensed broker, this guide will help you navigate the process with ease. Good luck on your journey to becoming a licensed real estate broker in California!

Preparing for the California Real Estate Broker Exam

Obtaining a real estate broker license in California is an important step towards advancing your career in the real estate industry. However, before you can become a licensed broker in the Golden State, you must pass the California Real Estate Broker Exam. This subchapter will guide you through the preparation process for this crucial exam.

To begin your preparation, it is essential to understand the exam's content and format. The California Real Estate Broker Exam consists of two parts: the National portion and the State-specific portion. The National portion covers topics such as property ownership, financing, contracts, and real estate practice. The State-specific portion focuses on California-specific laws and regulations.

To effectively prepare for the exam, consider enrolling in a reputable real estate school or taking an exam prep course. These resources will provide you with comprehensive study materials, practice exams, and guidance from experienced instructors. Additionally, they will help you navigate the complexities of California real estate laws and regulations.

Studying the California Real Estate Broker Exam content outline is crucial. This outline, available on the California Bureau of Real Estate's website, outlines the specific topics and subtopics that may be covered in the exam. Use this outline as a roadmap for your study plan, ensuring that you cover all the necessary material.

Practice exams are invaluable tools in your exam preparation. They allow you to familiarize yourself with the exam's format, identify areas of weakness, and build confidence in your knowledge. Many exam prep courses offer practice exams that closely resemble the actual California Real Estate Broker Exam. Take advantage of these resources to gauge your readiness and make any necessary adjustments to your study plan.

In addition to studying the exam content, it is crucial to develop effective test-taking strategies. Familiarize yourself with the exam's instructions and time limits. Practice time management techniques to ensure that you can answer all questions within the allocated time. Additionally, learn how to eliminate incorrect answer choices and make educated guesses when necessary.

Remember, preparation is key to success on the California Real Estate Broker Exam. Dedicate sufficient time and effort to studying the exam content, taking practice exams, and honing your test-taking skills. With proper preparation, you can confidently approach the exam and increase your chances of passing on your first attempt. Good luck!

Tips for a Successful Application Process in California

Applying for a real estate broker license in California can be a complex and time-consuming process. However, with the right guidance and preparation, you can navigate through it successfully. This subchapter provides valuable tips to help real estate agents and the public streamline their application process and increase their chances of obtaining a real estate broker license in the Golden State.

1. Familiarize Yourself with the Requirements: Before beginning the application process, it is crucial to understand the specific requirements set by the California Bureau of Real Estate. Thoroughly review the educational, experience, and examination prerequisites to ensure you meet all the criteria.

2. Complete the Necessary Education: California requires applicants to complete specific coursework before applying for a broker license. Make sure to enroll in an approved real estate education program that covers the required topics. Check the Bureau of Real Estate's website for a list of accredited institutions.

3. Gather Supporting Documents: As part of the application process, you will need to submit various supporting documents, such as proof of education, experience, and a completed application form. Gather these documents early on to avoid any delays in the application process.

4. Prepare for the Examination: California requires all broker license applicants to pass a state exam. Dedicate ample time to study and review the material covered in the exam. Consider enrolling in a prep course or utilizing study guides to enhance your chances of success.

5. Submit a Complete Application Package: Incomplete application packages can result in delays or even rejection of your application. Double-check that you have included all the required documents and information before submitting your application. Ensure that all forms are filled out correctly and any necessary fees are paid.

6. Stay Updated on the Application Status: Once you have submitted your application, regularly check the status online or contact the Bureau of Real Estate for updates. Be proactive in following up and addressing any additional requirements or inquiries promptly.

7. Seek Professional Assistance if Needed: If you find the application process overwhelming or confusing, consider seeking assistance from a real estate broker or a professional licensing service. They can guide you through the process, answer your questions, and help ensure you submit a complete and accurate application.

By following these tips, real estate agents and the public can navigate the California real estate broker license application process more efficiently.

Remember to stay organized, meet all the requirements, and seek help when necessary. Good luck on your journey to becoming a licensed real estate broker in California!

# Chapter 3: Step-by-Step Guide to Obtaining a Real Estate Broker License in Texas

Understanding the Texas Real Estate Broker License Requirements

Obtaining a real estate broker license in Texas can open up a world of opportunities for both real estate agents and the general public. However, navigating the requirements and application process can be complex and overwhelming without proper guidance. In this subchapter, we will delve into the essential information you need to know to understand the Texas real estate broker license requirements.

To become a licensed real estate broker in Texas, candidates must meet certain criteria set by the Texas Real Estate Commission (TREC). The first requirement is to have at least four years of active experience as a licensed real estate sales agent. This experience should be obtained within the past five years preceding the application.

Applicants must also complete 270 classroom hours of qualifying real estate courses, which include topics such as Principles of Real Estate, Law of Agency, and Law of Contracts. These courses can be taken at approved educational institutions, and a passing score on the final exams is necessary.

In addition to education and experience, applicants must submit fingerprints for a criminal background check. The TREC conducts these checks to ensure that only individuals of good moral character are granted a broker license.

Furthermore, candidates are required to complete the Broker Responsibility Course, a 6-hour course that covers the regulatory aspects of being a real estate broker.

Once these requirements are met, candidates can submit their application to the TREC along with the necessary fees. The application will be thoroughly reviewed, and if all requirements are satisfied, the candidate will be issued a real estate broker license.

Understanding the Texas real estate broker license requirements is crucial for both real estate agents and the public, as it ensures that only qualified individuals are practicing real estate brokerage in the state. By familiarizing yourself with these requirements, you can confidently pursue a career as a licensed real estate broker in Texas or make informed decisions when working with one.

Whether you are a real estate agent looking to advance your career or a member of the public seeking to understand the licensing process, this subchapter will serve as a valuable resource. By following the step-by-step approach outlined in this book, you can navigate the process of obtaining a real estate broker license in Texas and gain the knowledge necessary to succeed in the real estate industry.

Navigating the Application Process in Texas

Obtaining a real estate broker license in Texas can be a lucrative and fulfilling career choice for individuals interested in the real estate industry. However, the application process can be complex and time-consuming. This subchapter aims to provide a step-by-step guide to help real estate agents and the public navigate the application process in Texas smoothly.

Step 1: Meet the Eligibility Requirements

Before applying for a real estate broker license in Texas, it is crucial to ensure that you meet the eligibility requirements set by the Texas Real Estate Commission (TREC). These requirements typically include being at least 18 years old, having a high school diploma or equivalent, and completing a certain number of real estate courses.

Step 2: Complete the Required Education

To qualify for a real estate broker license in Texas, applicants must complete specific educational requirements. This usually involves completing a certain number of pre-licensing courses approved by the TREC. It is essential to research and enroll in a reputable real estate school that offers these courses.

Step 3: Prepare and Submit the Application

Once the educational requirements are fulfilled, applicants can begin preparing their license application. The TREC provides an online application system that simplifies the process. The application typically requires personal information, educational background, employment history, and any criminal history, if applicable. It is crucial to fill out the application accurately and attach all the necessary supporting documents.

Step 4: Schedule and Pass the State Exam

After submitting the application, applicants must schedule and pass the state exam administered by the TREC. The exam evaluates the applicant's knowledge of real estate laws, principles, and practices. Adequate preparation, such as studying relevant textbooks and taking practice exams, is essential for success.

Step 5: Obtain Errors and Omissions Insurance

Before receiving the broker license, applicants must obtain errors and omissions (E&O) insurance. This insurance protects brokers and their clients in case of any mistakes or negligence during transactions.

Step 6: Activate the Broker License

Once the broker license is granted, it is essential to activate the license by affiliating with a licensed Texas real estate brokerage. This affiliation allows brokers to legally engage in real estate transactions.

Navigating the application process in Texas can be overwhelming, but with the right guidance and preparation, it can be a smooth and successful journey. By following these steps, real estate agents and the public can confidently work towards obtaining their real estate broker license in Texas.

Preparing for the Texas Real Estate Broker Exam

Before taking the Texas Real Estate Broker Exam, it is important to properly prepare in order to increase your chances of success. This subchapter will outline the necessary steps and resources to help you study effectively and pass the exam with flying colors.

First and foremost, it is crucial to thoroughly review and understand the Texas Real Estate Licensing Act (TRELA) and the Texas Administrative Code (TAC). These are the primary sources of information that will be tested on the exam. Familiarize yourself with the rules, regulations, and laws that govern real estate transactions in Texas.

To enhance your understanding of these materials, consider enrolling in a pre-licensing course specifically designed for the Texas Real Estate Broker Exam. These courses are offered by various real estate schools and provide comprehensive instruction on the topics covered in the exam. They often include practice exams and study guides to help you prepare effectively.

In addition to the pre-licensing course, it is highly recommended to supplement your studies with additional exam prep materials. There are numerous online resources, study guides, and practice exams available that can help you become more familiar with the format and content of the Texas Real Estate Broker Exam.

One useful strategy is to form a study group with fellow real estate agents who are also preparing for the exam. Collaborating with others allows you to share knowledge, discuss difficult concepts, and quiz each other on key points. This can significantly enhance your understanding and retention of the material.

Furthermore, make sure to allocate sufficient time for regular study sessions. Creating a study schedule and sticking to it will help you stay organized and motivated. Set aside dedicated time each day to review the material, take practice exams, and reinforce your understanding of the topics.

Lastly, it is important to approach the exam with confidence and a positive mindset. Relaxation techniques such as deep breathing exercises and visualization can help reduce anxiety and improve focus. Remember to get a good night's sleep before the exam and arrive early to the testing center to ensure a smooth experience.

By following these steps and utilizing the available resources, you will be well-prepared for the Texas Real Estate Broker Exam. Good luck!

Tips for a Smooth Licensing Process in Texas

Obtaining a real estate broker license in Texas can be a complex process, but with the right guidance and preparation, you can navigate it smoothly. This subchapter aims to provide real estate agents and the public with valuable tips to ensure a seamless licensing process in the Lone Star State.

1. Familiarize Yourself with Requirements: Before diving into the licensing process, it is crucial to understand the specific requirements set by the Texas Real Estate Commission (TREC). These requirements may include education, experience, background checks, and passing the state exam. Make sure to thoroughly research and understand these prerequisites to avoid any surprises.

2. Complete Required Education: Texas requires aspiring brokers to complete specific education courses approved by TREC. Ensure that you enroll in a reputable real estate school or online platform that offers the necessary courses. Completing these courses diligently will equip you with the knowledge and skills needed to excel in your real estate career.

3. Seek Guidance from a Mentor: Finding a knowledgeable mentor who has successfully navigated the licensing process in Texas can greatly benefit you. They can provide valuable insights, answer your questions, and offer guidance throughout the journey. Building a mentorship relationship can help you avoid common pitfalls and make informed decisions along the way.

4. Prepare for the State Examination: Passing the state exam is a crucial step in obtaining your real estate broker license. Invest time and effort in studying relevant materials, taking practice tests, and familiarizing yourself with the exam format. Consider joining study groups or utilizing exam prep resources to enhance your chances of success.

5. Submit a Complete Application: When applying for your broker license, ensure that you have gathered all the necessary documents and information required by TREC. Pay close attention to details, as even minor omissions can delay the application process. Double-check your application to ensure accuracy and completeness before submitting it.

6. Maintain Open Communication: Throughout the licensing process, it is essential to maintain open communication with TREC and promptly respond to any requests or inquiries. Be proactive in providing any additional documentation or information as requested. This will help expedite the process and avoid unnecessary delays.

By following these tips, real estate agents and the public can enhance their chances of smoothly navigating the licensing process in Texas. Remember, preparation, diligence, and attention to detail are key to achieving success in obtaining a real estate broker license in the Lone Star State.

# Chapter 4: Navigating the Process of Getting a Real Estate Broker License in New York

Overview of the New York Real Estate Broker License Requirements

Obtaining a real estate broker license in New York can be a rewarding and lucrative career move. However, it is important to understand the specific requirements set forth by the state in order to obtain this license. In this subchapter, we will provide an overview of the New York real estate broker license requirements.

To become a licensed real estate broker in New York, there are several key prerequisites that applicants must meet. First and foremost, individuals must be at least 20 years old and have a high school diploma or its equivalent. Additionally, applicants must successfully complete a 75-hour real estate broker qualifying course approved by the New York State Department of State (NYSDOS).

After completing the education requirement, aspiring brokers must pass the New York State Real Estate Broker Examination. This exam evaluates the applicant's knowledge and understanding of various real estate topics, including agency relationships, real estate finance, property management, and New York state laws and regulations.

In addition to the educational and examination requirements, applicants must also gain practical experience in the real estate industry. This entails working as a licensed real estate salesperson under the supervision of a licensed real estate broker for a minimum of two years. During this time, individuals will gain valuable hands-on experience and learn the ins and outs of the industry.

Furthermore, applicants must provide proof of their legal presence and residency in the United States. This can be done by submitting various documents such as a driver's license, social security card, or passport.

Once all the requirements have been met, applicants can submit their license application to the NYSDOS along with the necessary fees. The application will be reviewed by the department, and if approved, the individual will receive their New York real estate broker license.

It is important to note that the real estate industry is regulated and subject to change. Therefore, it is crucial to stay up to date with any updates or modifications to the New York real estate broker license requirements. This can be done by regularly checking the NYSDOS website or consulting with a licensed real estate professional.

In conclusion, obtaining a real estate broker license in New York requires fulfilling specific requirements set forth by the state. By completing the educational course, passing the examination, gaining practical experience, and submitting the necessary documentation, individuals can embark on a rewarding career as a licensed real estate broker in the state of New York.

Step-by-Step Guide to Obtaining a Real Estate Broker License in New York

If you're interested in becoming a real estate broker in New York, you're in the right place. This step-by-step guide will walk you through the process of obtaining a real estate broker license in the Empire State.

Step 1: Meet the Requirements

Before you can apply for a real estate broker license in New York, you must meet certain requirements. These include being at least 20 years old, having a high school diploma or equivalent, and completing a

120-hour real estate broker training course approved by the New York Department of State.

Step 2: Gain Experience

To become a licensed real estate broker in New York, you must have at least two years of full-time real estate salesperson experience or equivalent part-time experience. Make sure to keep track of your transactions and maintain proof of your experience, as you'll need to submit this documentation with your application.

Step 3: Submit Your Application

Once you've met the requirements and gained the necessary experience, it's time to submit your application. You can find the application form on the New York Department of State's website. Make sure to complete all sections accurately and submit the required documentation, such as proof of experience and completion of the real estate broker training course.

Step 4: Pass the Examination

After submitting your application, you'll need to pass the New York State real estate broker examination. This exam tests your knowledge of real estate practices, laws, and regulations. Be sure to study and prepare for the exam to increase your chances of success.

Step 5: Obtain Sponsorship

To finalize your application, you'll need to obtain sponsorship from a licensed New York real estate broker. This broker will serve as your mentor and guide you through the early stages of your career. Make sure to choose a reputable and experienced broker who aligns with your professional goals.

Step 6: Receive Your License

Once you've completed all the steps and your application is approved, you'll receive your real estate broker license from the New York Department of State. Congratulations! You're now a licensed real estate broker in New York.

In conclusion, obtaining a real estate broker license in New York requires meeting the necessary requirements, gaining experience, submitting an application, passing an examination, obtaining sponsorship, and receiving your license. By following this step-by-step guide, you'll be on your way to a successful career as a real estate broker in the Empire State. Good luck!

Preparing for the New York Real Estate Broker Exam

The New York Real Estate Broker Exam is a crucial step towards obtaining your real estate broker license in the state. Whether you are a real estate agent looking to advance your career or a member of the public seeking to enter the industry, it is essential to be well-prepared for this exam. In this subchapter, we will guide you through the process of preparing for the New York Real Estate Broker Exam, ensuring that you have the knowledge and skills necessary to succeed.

To begin your preparation, it is crucial to familiarize yourself with the exam format and content. The New York Real Estate Broker Exam consists of multiple-choice questions that cover various topics, including real estate law, finance, property management, and ethics. Understanding the exam structure and content will help you focus your studies effectively.

Next, gather study materials that cover the exam topics comprehensively. The New York Department of State provides a Candidate Handbook that outlines the exam content and provides sample questions. Additionally, consider investing in reputable study guides and online resources to supplement your learning. These materials will help you gain a deeper understanding of the concepts and ensure you are well-prepared for the exam.

Creating a study plan is essential for efficient preparation. Allocate dedicated study time each day or week, depending on your schedule. Break down the exam topics into manageable sections and set specific goals for each study session. This will help you stay organized and ensure that you cover all the necessary content before the exam.

Practice exams are an invaluable tool for preparing for any exam, including the New York Real Estate Broker Exam. Many online platforms offer practice exams that simulate the actual test experience. Taking these practice exams will not only familiarize you with the exam format but also help you identify areas where you may need further study.

Lastly, consider joining study groups or seeking guidance from experienced real estate professionals. Engaging with others who are also preparing for the exam can provide valuable insights, study tips, and motivation. Additionally, reaching out to real estate brokers or professionals who have already passed the exam can provide you with firsthand advice and guidance for success.

In conclusion, preparing for the New York Real Estate Broker Exam requires a strategic approach. By familiarizing yourself with the exam content, gathering comprehensive study materials, creating a study plan, practicing with sample exams, and seeking guidance from professionals, you can increase your chances of passing the exam and obtaining your real estate broker license in New York.

Important Considerations for New York License Applicants

Obtaining a real estate broker license in New York can open up a world of opportunities for real estate agents looking to expand their career horizons. However, the process can be complex and overwhelming, requiring careful consideration and adherence to specific requirements. In this subchapter, we will explore the important considerations that all New York license applicants should keep in mind.

First and foremost, it is crucial to understand the eligibility criteria for obtaining a real estate broker license in New York. Applicants must be at least 20 years old and have successfully completed 120 hours of approved real estate education. Additionally, they must have at least two years of experience as a licensed real estate salesperson or three years of experience in the general real estate field.

One of the most critical aspects of the application process is the completion of the New York State Department of State's Application for Licensure as a Real Estate Broker. This application requires detailed information about an applicant's personal and professional background, including any criminal history or disciplinary actions. It is essential to provide accurate and complete information to avoid delays or potential denials.

Another consideration for New York license applicants is the requirement to pass the state licensing exam. This comprehensive exam covers various topics, including real estate law, agency relationships, financing, and property management. Adequate preparation and review of the exam content are crucial to ensure success.

Additionally, aspiring brokers must secure sponsorship from a licensed New York real estate broker. This sponsorship is necessary to activate the broker license and engage in real estate transactions. Building professional relationships and networking within the industry can greatly assist in finding a sponsoring broker.

Finally, it is important to note that obtaining a real estate broker license in New York comes with certain financial responsibilities. Applicants must pay the required fees, which include the application fee, license fee, and fingerprinting fee. Budgeting for these expenses is crucial to ensure a smooth application process.

In conclusion, aspiring real estate brokers in New York must carefully consider the eligibility criteria, application process, exam requirements, sponsorship, and financial obligations associated with obtaining a license. By understanding and addressing these important considerations, individuals can navigate the process with confidence and pave the way for a successful real estate career in the vibrant New York market.

# Chapter 5: Requirements for Obtaining a Real Estate Broker License in Florida

Understanding the Florida Real Estate Broker License Requirements

If you are considering becoming a real estate broker in the state of Florida, it is essential to understand the specific requirements and steps involved in obtaining your license. This subchapter will guide you through the process, ensuring you are well-informed and prepared for your journey.

To qualify for a real estate broker license in Florida, you must meet several criteria. Firstly, you must be at least 18 years old and have a high school diploma or its equivalent. Additionally, you must have a minimum of 24 months of real estate experience as a sales associate or have a four-year degree in real estate. It is important to note that this experience must be within the five years preceding your application.

Once you meet the experience requirement, you will need to complete a 72-hour pre-license education course approved by the Florida Real Estate Commission (FREC). This course covers various aspects of real estate, including laws, principles, and practices. After completing the course, you will receive a certificate of completion.

Next, you will need to pass the Florida Real Estate Broker Examination. This exam is administered by Pearson VUE and consists of both a state and national portion. The state portion covers Florida-specific laws and regulations, while the national portion covers general real estate concepts. It is crucial to thoroughly study and prepare for this exam, as it determines your eligibility for licensure.

Upon passing the examination, you will need to submit your application for a real estate broker license to the FREC. This application includes various documents such as proof of education, experience, and a background check. Additionally, you will need to pay the required fees.

Once your application is approved, you will be issued your real estate broker license. It is important to note that this license must be renewed every two years, and you must complete continuing education courses to maintain your licensure.

Understanding the Florida real estate broker license requirements is vital for anyone pursuing a career in the real estate industry. By following the steps outlined in this subchapter, you will be well-prepared to navigate the process and achieve your goal of becoming a licensed real estate broker in Florida. Good luck on your journey!

Step-by-Step Guide to Obtaining a Real Estate Broker License in Florida

If you're a real estate agent looking to take your career to the next level or a member of the public interested in becoming a real estate broker, this step-by-step guide will walk you through the process of obtaining a real estate broker license in Florida.

1. Understand the Requirements: Before you begin the application process, it's essential to familiarize yourself with the requirements set by the Florida Real Estate Commission (FREC). These requirements include being at least 18 years old, having a high school diploma or equivalent, and completing 24 months of real estate experience within the past five years.

2. Complete the Pre-Licensing Education: Florida requires 72 hours of pre-licensing education from an approved provider. This education covers topics such as real estate principles, laws, and practices. Make sure to choose a reputable and accredited provider to ensure your education meets the state's standards.

3. Submit the Application and Fees: Once you've completed the pre-licensing education, you can submit your application to the FREC. Along with the application, you'll need to include the required fees, which typically range from $105 to $205. It's crucial to double-check that you've included all necessary documents and fees to avoid any delays in processing.

4. Pass the State Exam: After your application is approved, you'll receive a notice to schedule your state exam. The exam consists of two parts: a national portion and a state-specific portion. You must pass both sections to obtain your broker license. Consider utilizing study materials and practice exams to increase your chances of success.

5. Secure a Broker Sponsor: In Florida, you must work under a licensed broker for a minimum of two years before you can become a broker yourself. Find a reputable broker who is willing to sponsor you during this period. This step allows you to gain valuable experience and knowledge in the industry.

6. Complete Post-Licensing Education: After passing the state exam, you must complete a 60-hour post-licensing course within the first year of licensure. This course covers topics such as brokerage management, real estate investment, and advanced real estate law.

7. Activate Your License: Once you've completed the post-licensing education, you can activate your real estate broker license. This involves submitting the required fees and documentation to the FREC. Upon approval, you can start practicing as a licensed real estate broker in Florida.

By following this step-by-step guide, you can navigate the process of obtaining a real estate broker license in Florida successfully. Remember to stay informed about the latest requirements and regulations set by the FREC to ensure a smooth and successful licensing journey. Good luck!

Preparing for the Florida Real Estate Broker Exam

Obtaining a real estate broker license in Florida is an important step in advancing your career in the real estate industry. To become a licensed broker in the Sunshine State, you must pass the Florida Real Estate Broker Exam. This subchapter will guide you through the preparation process for the exam, providing valuable tips and resources to maximize your chances of success.

The first step in preparing for the Florida Real Estate Broker Exam is to familiarize yourself with the exam content. The exam covers various topics, including real estate law, finance, appraisal, investment analysis, and property management. It is essential to review each topic thoroughly and ensure you have a solid understanding of the material.

One of the most effective ways to prepare for the exam is to enroll in a reputable real estate school or online course. These programs offer comprehensive study materials, practice exams, and expert guidance to help you navigate the exam successfully. Make sure to choose a program that is approved by the Florida Real Estate Commission (FREC) to ensure it meets the state's educational requirements.

In addition to formal education, self-study is also crucial for exam preparation. Create a study schedule and allocate sufficient time each day to review the exam topics. Utilize study guides, textbooks, and online resources to supplement your understanding of the material. Practice exams are particularly valuable as they simulate the actual exam experience and allow you to identify areas where you need to focus your studies.

Another essential aspect of exam preparation is staying up to date with current real estate laws and regulations in Florida. The FREC website is an excellent resource for accessing the latest information and updates.

Familiarize yourself with the Florida Statutes and Administrative Code governing real estate practices, as these will be tested on the exam.

Networking with experienced real estate brokers and professionals can also provide valuable insights and guidance during your exam preparation. Join local real estate associations, attend industry events, and participate in study groups to connect with knowledgeable individuals who can share their experiences and tips for success.

Lastly, maintaining a positive mindset and staying motivated throughout your exam preparation is vital. Remember that passing the Florida Real Estate Broker Exam is achievable with dedication and hard work. Stay focused, manage your time effectively, and approach the exam with confidence.

By following these preparation strategies, you will be well-equipped to tackle the Florida Real Estate Broker Exam and take the next step in your real estate career. Good luck!

Tips for a Successful Licensing Process in Florida

Obtaining a real estate broker license in Florida can open up numerous opportunities for real estate agents. However, the licensing process can be complex and overwhelming. To help you navigate through it successfully, here are some useful tips:

1. Understand the Requirements: The first step is to familiarize yourself with the requirements set by the Florida Real Estate Commission (FREC). These include completing the necessary pre-licensing education, passing the state exam, and meeting other eligibility criteria such as age and background checks.

2. Choose the Right Education Provider: Select a reputable real estate education provider that offers courses approved by FREC. These courses

will provide you with the knowledge and skills required to pass the state exam. Make sure to allocate sufficient time for studying and review.

3. Prepare for the State Exam: The state exam is a crucial step in the licensing process. Create a study schedule and utilize study materials, practice exams, and online resources to prepare effectively. Familiarize yourself with the exam format and content areas to focus your study efforts accordingly.

4. Complete the Application Process: Once you have completed the pre-licensing education and passed the state exam, you are ready to apply for your broker license. Submit a completed application along with the required documents, such as proof of education and exam results, to FREC. Ensure that you meet all the necessary deadlines and pay the application fee.

5. Consider Joining a Brokerage: While not mandatory, joining a reputable real estate brokerage can provide valuable guidance and support as you start your career as a licensed broker. Look for a brokerage that aligns with your professional goals and offers mentorship programs or training opportunities.

6. Maintain Continuing Education: After obtaining your broker license, it is essential to stay updated with industry trends and regulations. FREC requires licensed brokers to complete continuing education courses to renew their license. Stay informed about the latest courses and fulfill your continuing education requirements in a timely manner.

7. Network and Stay Engaged: Building a strong network is crucial in the real estate industry. Attend industry events, join professional organizations, and engage with fellow real estate agents to expand your connections and learn from experienced professionals. Stay up-to-date with market trends and changes in real estate laws and regulations.

By following these tips, you can enhance your chances of a successful licensing process in Florida. Remember to stay organized, dedicated, and proactive throughout the journey. Good luck on your path to becoming a licensed real estate broker in the Sunshine State!

# Chapter 6: How to Obtain a Real Estate Broker License in Illinois

Overview of the Illinois Real Estate Broker License Requirements

Obtaining a real estate broker license in Illinois is a crucial step towards a successful career in the real estate industry. Whether you are a real estate agent looking to expand your business or an aspiring professional seeking to enter the field, understanding the requirements and process for obtaining a broker license in Illinois is essential.

To become a licensed real estate broker in Illinois, you must fulfill several requirements set by the Illinois Department of Financial and Professional Regulation (IDFPR). Firstly, you must be at least 21 years old and possess a high school diploma or equivalent. Additionally, you must complete 90 hours of pre-license education from an approved real estate school. This education includes topics such as real estate principles, practices, and Illinois laws and regulations.

After completing the pre-license education, you must pass the Illinois Real Estate Broker Examination administered by the IDFPR. The exam consists of both national and state-specific sections, covering various aspects of real estate practices and laws in Illinois. It is crucial to thoroughly study and prepare for the exam to increase your chances of success.

Once you pass the examination, you must submit an application for your broker license to the IDFPR. This application requires you to provide personal information, education details, and any relevant work experience. Additionally, you must submit fingerprints for a criminal background check.

To complete the licensing process, you must also obtain a sponsoring broker. A sponsoring broker is an experienced real estate professional who will mentor and supervise you during your early years as a broker. This relationship is crucial for gaining practical knowledge and experience in the field.

Throughout your career as a licensed real estate broker in Illinois, you must renew your license every two years. The renewal process requires completing continuing education courses, which help you stay updated on industry trends, changes in laws and regulations, and best practices.

In conclusion, obtaining a real estate broker license in Illinois requires meeting specific requirements, including completing pre-license education, passing an examination, and finding a sponsoring broker. By understanding and fulfilling these requirements, you can embark on a successful journey in the Illinois real estate industry.

Step-by-Step Guide to Obtaining a Real Estate Broker License in Illinois

Congratulations on taking the first step towards becoming a licensed real estate broker in the state of Illinois! Obtaining a broker license can open up countless opportunities for your career, allowing you to take on more responsibilities and increase your earning potential. In this chapter, we will provide you with a step-by-step guide to help you navigate the process of obtaining a real estate broker license in Illinois.

Step 1: Meet the Requirements

Before you can apply for a broker license in Illinois, you must meet several requirements. These include being at least 21 years old, having a high school diploma or equivalent, completing a 90-hour pre-license education course, and passing the state licensing exam.

Step 2: Complete the Pre-License Education

To fulfill the pre-license education requirement, you must complete a 90-hour course approved by the Illinois Department of Financial and Professional Regulation (IDFPR). This course covers various topics, including real estate principles, practices, and laws.

Step 3: Pass the State Licensing Exam

After completing the pre-license education, you must pass the state licensing exam administered by the IDFPR. The exam consists of both national and state-specific sections, testing your knowledge of real estate principles, laws, and practices.

Step 4: Apply for Your License

Once you have passed the exam, you can apply for your broker license through the IDFPR's online licensing system. You will need to submit an application, pay the required fees, and provide any additional documentation requested.

Step 5: Complete the Post-License Education

Within the first year of obtaining your broker license, you must complete a 30-hour post-license education course. This course is designed to provide you with additional knowledge and skills necessary for success as a real estate broker.

Step 6: Maintain Your License

To maintain your broker license in Illinois, you must renew it every two years. This includes completing continuing education requirements, which consist of 12 hours of approved coursework.

By following this step-by-step guide, you can successfully obtain your real estate broker license in Illinois. Remember, the process may take time and effort, but the rewards are well worth it. Good luck on your journey to becoming a licensed real estate broker in the great state of Illinois!

Preparing for the Illinois Real Estate Broker Exam

If you're looking to become a licensed real estate broker in Illinois, it's important to thoroughly prepare for the state's broker exam. This subchapter will guide you through the process, providing you with the necessary information and resources to succeed.

The first step in preparing for the Illinois Real Estate Broker Exam is to understand the exam's content and format. The exam consists of two portions: the national portion and the state-specific portion. The national portion covers topics such as property ownership, contracts, finance, and real estate calculations. The state-specific portion focuses on Illinois-specific laws and regulations.

To study for the exam, it's recommended to use a comprehensive study guide that covers both the national and state-specific portions. The Illinois Department of Financial and Professional Regulation (IDFPR) provides a list of approved study materials on their website. These study guides often include practice exams and review questions to help you test your knowledge and identify areas that need improvement.

In addition to using study guides, consider enrolling in a pre-licensing course. These courses are designed to provide you with a thorough understanding of the real estate industry and prepare you for the exam. Many reputable real estate schools offer online or in-person courses that cater to different learning styles and schedules.

Another important aspect of preparing for the Illinois Real Estate Broker Exam is familiarizing yourself with the state's real estate laws and regulations. The IDFPR website provides access to the Illinois Real Estate License Act and other relevant statutes and rules. Take the time to review these documents and make note of any important information that may be tested on the exam.

Lastly, don't underestimate the value of practice exams. Taking practice exams will not only help you become familiar with the format and content of the actual exam but also improve your test-taking skills. Many online platforms offer practice exams specifically tailored to the Illinois Real Estate Broker Exam.

In conclusion, preparing for the Illinois Real Estate Broker Exam requires a comprehensive approach. Utilize approved study materials, consider enrolling in a pre-licensing course, familiarize yourself with state laws and regulations, and take practice exams. By following these steps, you'll increase your chances of success on the exam and ultimately obtaining your real estate broker license in Illinois.

Important Considerations for Illinois License Applicants

When it comes to obtaining a real estate broker license in Illinois, there are several important considerations that both real estate agents and the public should keep in mind. Understanding these considerations can make the application process smoother and increase the chances of success. In this subchapter, we will discuss the key factors that Illinois license applicants need to be aware of.

First and foremost, it is crucial to meet the basic eligibility requirements set by the Illinois Department of Financial and Professional Regulation (IDFPR). These requirements include being at least 21 years old, having a high school diploma or equivalent, and completing the required education courses. Applicants must also pass a state-administered exam and undergo a background check.

One important consideration for Illinois license applicants is the need to choose a sponsoring broker. In Illinois, all real estate licensees must work under the supervision of a licensed sponsoring broker. It is essential to find a sponsoring broker who aligns with your professional goals and provides the necessary support and mentorship throughout your career.

Another factor to consider is the cost associated with obtaining a real estate broker license in Illinois. Applicants should be prepared to pay for the required education courses, exam fees, and licensing fees. It is essential to budget for these expenses and factor them into your overall plan.

Additionally, Illinois license applicants should familiarize themselves with the state's real estate laws and regulations. Understanding the legal framework in which you will operate as a real estate broker is crucial for success and compliance. It is recommended to stay updated on any changes or updates in the Illinois real estate industry to ensure you are providing accurate and reliable information to your clients.

Lastly, networking and building relationships within the Illinois real estate community can significantly benefit license applicants. Attending industry events, joining professional associations, and connecting with experienced brokers can provide valuable insights, mentorship, and potential business opportunities.

In conclusion, obtaining a real estate broker license in Illinois requires careful consideration of eligibility requirements, finding a sponsoring broker, budgeting for associated costs, understanding state laws and regulations, and networking within the industry. By taking these important considerations into account, aspiring license applicants can navigate the process more effectively and increase their chances of success in the Illinois real estate market.

# Chapter 7: Guide to Getting a Real Estate Broker License in Pennsylvania

Understanding the Pennsylvania Real Estate Broker License Requirements

Obtaining a real estate broker license in Pennsylvania is an important step towards advancing your career in the real estate industry. Whether you are a seasoned real estate agent looking to take the next step or someone completely new to the field, understanding the requirements for obtaining a broker license in Pennsylvania is crucial. This subchapter will provide you with a comprehensive overview of the Pennsylvania real estate broker license requirements.

To become a licensed real estate broker in Pennsylvania, you must meet certain eligibility criteria. Firstly, you must be at least 21 years old and have a high school diploma or equivalent. Additionally, you must have successfully completed 240 hours of approved real estate education, which includes various topics such as real estate law, ethics, finance, and more.

Once you have completed the required education, you will need to pass the Pennsylvania Real Estate Broker Examination. This examination assesses your knowledge of real estate laws, regulations, and practices specific to Pennsylvania. It is essential to thoroughly prepare for the exam by studying relevant materials and taking practice tests to increase your chances of success.

In addition to education and examination, there are other requirements that must be fulfilled. You must provide evidence of at least three years of experience as a licensed real estate salesperson or equivalent. This experience should involve actively engaging in real estate transactions.

Furthermore, you must submit a completed application along with the necessary fees to the Pennsylvania Real Estate Commission.

It is important to note that Pennsylvania also requires real estate brokers to maintain professional liability insurance coverage. This insurance protects brokers against claims arising from errors, omissions, or negligence in their professional services.

Understanding the Pennsylvania real estate broker license requirements is vital for both real estate agents and the public. Real estate agents can use this information to plan their career progression and take the necessary steps to obtain a broker license. On the other hand, the public can benefit from understanding these requirements when choosing a qualified and licensed real estate broker to represent their interests in real estate transactions.

Overall, obtaining a real estate broker license in Pennsylvania requires a combination of education, experience, examination, and application. By fulfilling these requirements, you will be well on your way to becoming a licensed real estate broker in the state of Pennsylvania.

Step-by-Step Guide to Obtaining a Real Estate Broker License in Pennsylvania

Pennsylvania is a state with a thriving real estate market, making it an attractive place for individuals looking to become licensed real estate brokers. If you're interested in pursuing a career in real estate brokerage in Pennsylvania, this step-by-step guide will walk you through the process.

1. Meet the eligibility criteria: Before applying for a real estate broker license in Pennsylvania, ensure that you meet the eligibility criteria. You must be at least 21 years old, have a high school diploma or equivalent, and have completed 240 hours of approved real estate education.

2. Complete the required education: Pennsylvania requires aspiring real estate brokers to complete 240 hours of approved real estate education. This education should cover topics such as real estate law, finance, appraisal, and ethics. You can find approved education providers on the Pennsylvania Real Estate Commission (PREC) website.

3. Gain real estate experience: To qualify for a broker license, you must have at least three years of experience as a licensed salesperson or a combination of education and experience. Document your experience and keep track of the transactions you were involved in.

4. Submit the application: Once you have completed the education and gained the necessary experience, you can submit your application for a real estate broker license to the PREC. The application includes a fee, proof of education and experience, and a criminal background check.

5. Pass the state exam: After your application is reviewed and approved, you will need to pass the Pennsylvania real estate broker examination. The exam covers various topics related to real estate brokerage, including state-specific laws and regulations.

6. Find a sponsoring broker: In Pennsylvania, real estate brokers must work under the supervision of a sponsoring broker. Find a reputable broker who is willing to sponsor and mentor you as you start your career as a broker.

7. Activate your license: Once you have passed the exam and found a sponsoring broker, you can activate your real estate broker license. Pay the required fees and complete any additional paperwork to officially become a licensed real estate broker in Pennsylvania.

Remember, the process of obtaining a real estate broker license in Pennsylvania may have additional requirements or steps that are not covered in this guide. It's important to consult the PREC website or contact them directly for the most up-to-date and accurate information.

Becoming a licensed real estate broker in Pennsylvania can open doors to a rewarding and lucrative career in the real estate industry. Follow this step-by-step guide to navigate the process successfully and embark on your journey as a licensed real estate broker in the Keystone State.

Preparing for the Pennsylvania Real Estate Broker Exam

If you are considering obtaining a real estate broker license in Pennsylvania, it is important to be well-prepared for the state exam. This subchapter will guide you through the necessary steps to ensure a successful outcome.

First and foremost, familiarize yourself with the Pennsylvania Real Estate Commission's requirements for becoming a licensed broker. These requirements typically include being at least 21 years old, having a minimum of three years of real estate salesperson experience, completing an approved broker education program, and passing the state exam. Make sure you meet all the prerequisites before proceeding.

To begin your preparation, enroll in a reputable real estate broker education program. These programs are designed to provide you with the knowledge and skills necessary to pass the exam and succeed in your future career. Look for programs that are approved by the Pennsylvania Real Estate Commission and offer comprehensive coverage of the exam topics.

Once you have completed the education program, it is time to schedule your exam. The Pennsylvania Real Estate Commission administers the exam through a third-party testing provider. Visit their website to find out the available dates and locations for the exam. Be sure to register well in advance to secure your preferred date and location.

To increase your chances of success, consider investing in exam preparation materials such as practice exams and study guides. These resources will help you familiarize yourself with the format and content of the exam, as well as identify areas where you may need additional study.

Additionally, take advantage of any available exam preparation courses or workshops. These resources are often offered by real estate schools or professional associations and can provide valuable insights and strategies for tackling the exam.

As the exam date approaches, create a study schedule and stick to it. Dedicate specific time each day to review the material and practice answering sample questions. This will help you build confidence and improve your test-taking skills.

On the day of the exam, arrive early and bring all the required identification and materials. Stay calm and focused during the exam, and carefully read each question before selecting your answer. Remember to manage your time wisely to ensure you have enough time to answer all the questions.

After completing the exam, you will receive your results immediately. If you pass, congratulations! You can now proceed with the application process for your Pennsylvania real estate broker license. If you do not pass, don't be discouraged. Use your exam results to identify areas where you need improvement and consider retaking the exam after additional study and preparation.

In conclusion, preparing for the Pennsylvania Real Estate Broker Exam requires careful planning, dedication, and thorough study. By following the steps outlined in this subchapter, you will be well-prepared to pass the exam and take the next steps towards obtaining your Pennsylvania real estate broker license. Good luck!

Tips for a Smooth Licensing Process in Pennsylvania

Obtaining a real estate broker license in Pennsylvania can be a complex process, but with the right guidance and knowledge, it can be a smooth and successful journey. In this subchapter, we will provide you with essential tips that will help you navigate through the licensing process in Pennsylvania with ease.

1. Familiarize yourself with the requirements: Before starting the licensing process, it is crucial to understand the requirements set by the Pennsylvania Real Estate Commission (PREC). Make sure you meet the educational and experience prerequisites to avoid any delays or setbacks.

2. Complete the required education: Pennsylvania requires prospective brokers to complete 240 hours of approved real estate education. Ensure you enroll in an accredited institution that offers the necessary courses to meet this requirement. It's also important to keep track of your transcripts and certificates for future reference.

3. Prepare for the licensing exam: The next step is to prepare for and pass the Pennsylvania real estate broker licensing exam. Study diligently and utilize practice exams and study materials to improve your chances of success. Familiarize yourself with the exam format, content, and time constraints to feel confident on exam day.

4. Submit your application: Once you have successfully passed the licensing exam, it's time to submit your broker license application to the PREC. Double-check the application form, attach all required documents, and pay the necessary fees. Be prepared for a background check and fingerprinting as part of the application process.

5. Establish a brokerage relationship: As a licensed real estate broker in Pennsylvania, you must work under the supervision of a licensed real estate broker or establish your own brokerage firm. Determine the best option for your career goals and start building your network within the industry.

6. Continuing education: To maintain your broker license in Pennsylvania, you will need to complete continuing education courses periodically. Stay informed about the latest requirements and ensure you fulfill them to keep your license active.

7. Stay updated on real estate regulations: Real estate regulations are subject to change, and it's essential to stay updated on any new laws or regulations that may affect your practice. Regularly check the PREC's website and participate in industry events and seminars to stay informed.

By following these tips, you can streamline the licensing process and embark on a successful real estate career in Pennsylvania. Remember to seek guidance from experienced professionals and utilize available resources to ensure a smooth journey towards obtaining your real estate broker license.

# Chapter 8: Steps to Becoming a Licensed Real Estate Broker in Georgia

Overview of the Georgia Real Estate Broker License Requirements

Obtaining a real estate broker license in Georgia is an important step for individuals looking to advance their careers in the real estate industry. Whether you are a real estate agent looking to take on more responsibilities or a member of the public interested in becoming a licensed broker, understanding the requirements for obtaining a broker license in Georgia is crucial.

To become a licensed real estate broker in Georgia, you must meet certain criteria set by the Georgia Real Estate Commission (GREC). First and foremost, you must be at least 21 years old and have a high school diploma or its equivalent. Additionally, you must have successfully completed a 60-hour Georgia broker pre-license course from a GREC-approved education provider.

After completing the pre-license course, you must pass the Georgia Real Estate Broker Examination. This examination tests your knowledge of real estate principles and practices, as well as Georgia-specific laws and regulations. It is important to thoroughly study and prepare for this exam to ensure success.

Once you have passed the examination, you must submit an application for a real estate broker license to the GREC. The application includes providing proof of completion of the pre-license course and passing the examination, as well as submitting to a criminal background check. It is important to disclose any criminal history, as failure to do so may result in denial of your application.

In addition to these requirements, you must also meet the experience requirement set by the GREC. To qualify for a broker license, you must have at least three years of active real estate salesperson or broker experience within the past five years. This experience requirement can be satisfied through documented transactions and employment history.

Once your application is approved, you will be issued a Georgia real estate broker license. This license allows you to engage in real estate brokerage activities, such as representing buyers and sellers, leasing or renting properties, and negotiating contracts.

In conclusion, obtaining a real estate broker license in Georgia requires completing a pre-license course, passing an examination, meeting the experience requirement, and submitting an application to the Georgia Real Estate Commission. By successfully navigating these requirements, you can take your real estate career to the next level and enjoy the benefits and opportunities that come with being a licensed broker in Georgia.

Step-by-Step Guide to Obtaining a Real Estate Broker License in Georgia

If you're considering a career as a real estate broker in Georgia, it's important to understand the requirements and steps involved in obtaining your license. This step-by-step guide will walk you through the process, ensuring you have all the information you need to successfully navigate the application process.

1. Meet the eligibility requirements: Before applying for a real estate broker license in Georgia, you must meet certain eligibility criteria. This includes being at least 21 years old, having a high school diploma or equivalent, and completing a pre-license education course approved by the Georgia Real Estate Commission (GREC).

2. Complete the pre-license education course: Georgia requires aspiring real estate brokers to complete a 60-hour pre-license education course. This course covers topics such as agency relationships, contracts, real estate finance, and Georgia real estate law. Make sure to choose a course approved by the GREC.

3. Pass the broker exam: Once you've completed the pre-license education course, you'll need to pass the Georgia broker exam. This exam is administered by PSI Exams and consists of both national and state-specific portions. Study materials and practice exams are available to help you prepare for the exam.

4. Obtain sponsorship: In Georgia, you must have a sponsoring broker before you can apply for your license. This means finding a real estate brokerage firm that is willing to sponsor you. The sponsoring broker will provide you with the necessary support and supervision as you begin your career.

5. Submit your application: After passing the broker exam and securing a sponsoring broker, you can submit your application for a real estate broker license to the GREC. The application includes a fee, proof of completing the pre-license education course, passing exam scores, and a criminal background check.

6. Complete the post-license education: Once your application is approved, you will need to complete a 25-hour post-license education course within the first year of receiving your license. This course covers important topics such as trust accounts, fair housing laws, and agency relationships.

7. Maintain your license: To maintain your real estate broker license in Georgia, you must renew it every four years. This requires completing continuing education courses approved by the GREC and paying the renewal fee.

By following this step-by-step guide, you'll be well on your way to obtaining a real estate broker license in Georgia. Remember to stay organized, study diligently for the exam, and seek support from experienced professionals in the industry. Good luck on your journey to becoming a licensed real estate broker in the Peach State!

Preparing for the Georgia Real Estate Broker Exam

Obtaining a real estate broker license in Georgia is a significant achievement that can open doors to a rewarding and lucrative career. However, before you can embark on this journey, you must successfully pass the Georgia Real Estate Broker Exam. This subchapter will guide both real estate agents and the public on how to prepare effectively for this crucial examination.

The Georgia Real Estate Broker Exam is a comprehensive test that evaluates your knowledge and understanding of real estate laws, practices, and ethics. To ensure you are adequately prepared, it is essential to follow a systematic approach.

First and foremost, familiarize yourself with the exam content. The Georgia Real Estate Commission provides a detailed outline of the topics covered in the exam. Reviewing this outline will help you identify areas where you may require additional study and focus.

Next, gather study materials that cover the exam content comprehensively. Look for reputable textbooks, online resources, and practice exams specifically designed for the Georgia Real Estate Broker Exam. These resources will provide you with the necessary knowledge and practice questions to sharpen your understanding and test-taking skills.

Consider enrolling in a pre-licensing course or a broker exam prep course. These courses are designed to provide in-depth instruction on the exam content, exam-taking strategies, and tips for success. They often include interactive exercises, mock exams, and expert guidance to help you feel confident and well-prepared.

Create a study schedule that suits your learning style and commitments. Dedicate regular time slots for studying and stick to your schedule consistently. Break down the exam content into manageable sections and allocate specific study time for each topic. This approach will ensure you cover all the necessary material without feeling overwhelmed.

Join study groups or find a study partner. Collaborating with others who are also preparing for the Georgia Real Estate Broker Exam can be extremely beneficial. Discussing concepts, asking questions, and sharing resources can deepen your understanding and provide valuable insights.

Lastly, take advantage of online forums and discussion boards dedicated to real estate exam preparation. These platforms allow you to connect with individuals who have already passed the exam or are also preparing for it. You can seek advice, share study tips, and gain encouragement from others who are on the same journey.

Remember, success in the Georgia Real Estate Broker Exam requires dedication, discipline, and thorough preparation. By following these guidelines, real estate agents and the public can significantly enhance their chances of passing the exam and obtaining their broker license in the state of Georgia. Good luck!

Important Considerations for Georgia License Applicants

Obtaining a real estate broker license in Georgia can be a rewarding and lucrative career move. However, it is important for license applicants to understand the specific requirements and considerations unique to this state. This subchapter will guide real estate agents and the public through the essential steps and considerations for obtaining a real estate broker license in Georgia.

One of the first considerations for Georgia license applicants is the educational requirements. To be eligible for a broker license, applicants must complete a minimum of 60 hours of approved real estate courses. These courses cover various topics, including real estate principles, finance, and Georgia law. It is crucial for applicants to choose an accredited educational institution that offers these courses and ensure they complete the required hours.

Another crucial consideration is the experience requirement. In Georgia, applicants must have at least three years of active experience as a licensed salesperson or broker during the five years preceding the application. This experience must be substantiated with proper documentation, such as commission statements or employment verification.

Additionally, applicants must pass the Georgia broker examination. This exam tests the applicant's knowledge of real estate principles, practices, and laws specific to Georgia. It is essential for applicants to thoroughly study and prepare for this exam to increase their chances of success.

Furthermore, Georgia license applicants must submit a completed application, along with the necessary fees and supporting documents, to the Georgia Real Estate Commission (GREC). These supporting documents may include proof of education, experience, and a criminal background check. It is vital for applicants to carefully review the application requirements and ensure all documents are accurate and up to date.

Lastly, it is important for license applicants to understand the ongoing obligations and responsibilities of a licensed broker in Georgia. This includes maintaining proper records, complying with ethical guidelines, and continuously updating their knowledge of real estate laws and regulations.

In conclusion, obtaining a real estate broker license in Georgia requires careful consideration of the educational requirements, experience, examination, application process, and ongoing obligations. By understanding and fulfilling these requirements, real estate agents and the public can take the necessary steps towards becoming a licensed real estate broker in Georgia.

# Chapter 9: Understanding the Process of Getting a Real Estate Broker License in Ohio

Overview of the Ohio Real Estate Broker License Requirements

In the state of Ohio, obtaining a real estate broker license is an important step for those looking to advance their careers in the real estate industry. Whether you are a real estate agent or a member of the public interested in becoming a licensed broker, it is crucial to understand the requirements and steps involved in obtaining a real estate broker license in Ohio.

To become a licensed real estate broker in Ohio, there are several key requirements that must be met. First, applicants must be at least 18 years old and have a high school diploma or equivalent. Additionally, they must complete a minimum of 120 hours of approved real estate education, which includes courses in real estate principles and practices, law, finance, and appraisal.

After completing the required education, applicants must pass the Ohio Real Estate Broker Exam. This exam consists of both a national portion and a state-specific portion, covering topics such as real estate law, contracts, financing, and ethics. It is important to note that passing the exam is just one step in the process and does not guarantee a broker license.

In addition to education and passing the exam, applicants must also gain practical experience in the real estate field. To qualify for a broker license, individuals must have at least two years of active experience as a licensed real estate salesperson or broker within the past five years. This experience must be verified by a licensed broker or salesperson who has supervised the applicant.

Once all the requirements have been met, applicants can submit their broker license application to the Ohio Division of Real Estate and Professional Licensing. The application includes a fee, proof of completing the required education, exam scores, and documentation of the required experience.

It is important to keep in mind that the process of obtaining a real estate broker license in Ohio can be complex and time-consuming. Therefore, it is recommended to thoroughly research the requirements and seek guidance from experienced professionals in the industry.

By understanding the overview of Ohio's real estate broker license requirements, both real estate agents and the public can gain valuable insights into the steps involved in becoming a licensed broker in the state. This knowledge can help individuals navigate the process more effectively and take the necessary steps towards achieving their goals in the real estate industry.

Step-by-Step Guide to Obtaining a Real Estate Broker License in Ohio

If you're considering a career as a real estate broker in Ohio, it's important to understand the steps involved in obtaining your license. This step-by-step guide will provide you with a clear overview of the requirements and application process in Ohio.

Step 1: Meet the Eligibility Criteria

Before applying for a real estate broker license in Ohio, you must meet certain eligibility criteria. To qualify, you must be at least 18 years old, have a high school diploma or equivalent, and complete a 120-hour pre-licensing education program from an approved provider.

Step 2: Gain Experience as a Salesperson

To become a broker in Ohio, you must first gain experience as a real estate salesperson. You must have actively engaged in the real estate business for at least two years as a licensed salesperson in Ohio or another state.

Step 3: Complete the Required Education

In addition to the pre-licensing education program, you must complete a 20-hour advanced principles and practices course approved by the Ohio Division of Real Estate and Professional Licensing. This course provides you with the necessary knowledge and skills to operate as a real estate broker.

Step 4: Submit Your Application

Once you have met the eligibility requirements and completed the necessary education, you can submit your application for a real estate broker license. The application must include proof of completing the required education, evidence of your experience as a salesperson, and the appropriate fees.

Step 5: Pass the Examination

After submitting your application, you will need to pass the Ohio real estate broker examination. This exam tests your knowledge of real estate laws, practices, and principles. You must achieve a minimum score of 75% to pass.

Step 6: Obtain Errors and Omissions Insurance

Before your license can be issued, you must obtain errors and omissions insurance. This insurance protects you and your clients from potential errors or omissions in your professional services.

Step 7: Activate Your License

Once you have completed all the necessary steps and obtained your real estate broker license, you can activate your license. This involves finding a sponsoring broker who will supervise your activities and ensure compliance with Ohio real estate laws.

By following this step-by-step guide, you can successfully obtain your real estate broker license in Ohio. Remember to familiarize yourself with the specific requirements and guidelines set forth by the Ohio Division of Real Estate and Professional Licensing to ensure a smooth and efficient application process. Good luck on your journey to becoming a licensed real estate broker in Ohio!

Preparing for the Ohio Real Estate Broker Exam

If you're considering a career as a real estate broker in Ohio, it's essential to understand the steps involved in obtaining your license. One crucial aspect of this process is preparing for the Ohio Real Estate Broker Exam. This subchapter will guide you through the necessary steps to ensure you are well-prepared for the exam.

The Ohio Real Estate Broker Exam is designed to test your knowledge and understanding of the real estate industry, laws, regulations, and ethical practices. To increase your chances of passing the exam, it's important to dedicate sufficient time and effort to your preparation.

First and foremost, familiarize yourself with the exam format and content. The Ohio Division of Real Estate and Professional Licensing provides an exam content outline that highlights the key topics you need to study. This outline will serve as your study guide and will help you structure your preparation.

Next, gather study materials that cover the content outlined by the Ohio Division of Real Estate and Professional Licensing. These materials may include textbooks, online courses, practice exams, and study guides. It's essential to choose reputable sources that align with Ohio's real estate laws and regulations.

Create a study schedule that allows you to cover all the necessary topics within a reasonable timeframe. Break down your study sessions into manageable chunks and allocate specific time slots for each topic. Consistency is key, so make sure to stick to your study schedule.

Consider joining a study group or finding a study partner. Collaborating with others who are also preparing for the exam can be beneficial as you can share knowledge, clarify doubts, and motivate one another.

Take advantage of practice exams to assess your knowledge and identify areas where you need improvement. These exams will help familiarize you with the exam format and simulate real exam conditions. Make sure to review your answers and understand the rationale behind each correct answer.

Lastly, maintain a healthy lifestyle during your preparation period. Get enough sleep, exercise regularly, and eat nutritious meals. Taking care of your physical and mental well-being will optimize your learning capacity and improve your overall performance.

In conclusion, preparing for the Ohio Real Estate Broker Exam requires dedication, organization, and thorough study. By following the steps outlined in this subchapter, you'll be well-equipped to tackle the exam with confidence and increase your chances of obtaining your real estate broker license in Ohio. Good luck!

Tips for a Successful Licensing Process in Ohio

Obtaining a real estate broker license in Ohio can be a rewarding and lucrative career move. However, the licensing process can seem overwhelming, especially if you are not familiar with the requirements and steps involved. In this subchapter, we will provide you with valuable tips to navigate the process and increase your chances of success.

1. Understand the Requirements: Before starting the licensing process, it is crucial to familiarize yourself with Ohio's specific requirements. These may include completing pre-licensing education, passing a state exam, and meeting certain experience criteria. Researching and understanding these requirements will help you plan and prepare accordingly.

2. Choose a Reputable Education Provider: To meet the pre-licensing education requirement, it is essential to select a reputable education provider. Look for providers that offer comprehensive and up-to-date coursework, as well as resources to help you succeed in the state exam. Consider online options for flexibility and convenience.

3. Prepare for the State Exam: The state exam is a crucial step in obtaining your real estate broker license. To increase your chances of success, dedicate sufficient time to study and review the exam material. Utilize practice exams and study guides to familiarize yourself with the format and content.

4. Build a Strong Network: Networking is vital in the real estate industry, and Ohio is no exception. Start building relationships with other real estate professionals, attend industry events, and join local real estate associations. Networking can provide valuable opportunities for mentorship, referrals, and career growth.

5. Stay Updated on Ohio Real Estate Laws: Ohio's real estate laws and regulations can change over time. It is essential to stay updated on these changes to ensure compliance and provide the best service to your clients. Follow reputable industry publications, attend continuing education courses, and participate in professional development opportunities.

6. Seek Guidance from a Mentor: Finding a mentor who is experienced in the Ohio real estate market can be immensely helpful. A mentor can provide guidance, share valuable insights, and help you navigate challenges along the way. Look for mentors who have a track record of success and are willing to invest in your professional growth.

By following these tips, you can streamline your licensing process and increase your chances of success in Ohio's real estate industry. Remember to stay organized, be proactive in your education, and seek support from industry professionals. Good luck on your journey to obtaining a real estate broker license in Ohio!

# Chapter 10: Requirements and Application Process for a Real Estate Broker License in Virginia

Understanding the Virginia Real Estate Broker License Requirements

Obtaining a real estate broker license in Virginia is an important step for individuals looking to advance their real estate careers. Whether you are a real estate agent or a member of the public interested in becoming a broker, it is crucial to understand the specific requirements set forth by the Virginia Real Estate Board. This subchapter will provide you with a comprehensive overview of the Virginia real estate broker license requirements, guiding you through the necessary steps to achieve your goal.

To become a licensed real estate broker in Virginia, you must first meet the following prerequisites:

1. Age Requirement: You must be at least 18 years old to apply for a real estate broker license in Virginia.

2. Experience: A minimum of 36 months (or equivalent) of active experience as a licensed salesperson or broker is required. This experience must be obtained within the past 10 years.

3. Education: Completion of 180 hours of pre-licensing education from a state-approved real estate school is mandatory. These courses cover topics such as real estate law, finance, contracts, and agency relationships.

4. Examination: You must pass the Virginia Real Estate Broker Examination, which tests your knowledge of state-specific real estate laws and regulations. The exam consists of both national and state-specific components.

5. Criminal Background Check: All applicants are required to undergo a criminal background check conducted by the Virginia State Police.

Once you have met these prerequisites, you can begin the application process. The Virginia Real Estate Board requires applicants to submit a completed application form, along with the necessary supporting documents, such as proof of education, experience, and examination results. Additionally, you will need to pay the required application and licensing fees.

It is crucial to note that maintaining a real estate broker license in Virginia requires continuing education. Brokers must complete 24 hours of continuing education courses every two years to stay current with industry changes and maintain their license.

Understanding the Virginia real estate broker license requirements is essential for both real estate agents and the general public. By following the step-by-step approach outlined in this subchapter, you can navigate the application process with confidence and work towards achieving your real estate broker license in Virginia.

Step-by-Step Guide to Obtaining a Real Estate Broker License in Virginia

If you are considering a career as a real estate broker in Virginia, you need to understand the specific requirements and steps involved in obtaining your license. This step-by-step guide will walk you through the process, ensuring that you have all the information you need to successfully navigate the application process.

1. Meet the basic eligibility requirements: In Virginia, you must be at least 18 years old, have a high school diploma or equivalent, and be a U.S. citizen or legal resident.

2. Complete the required pre-licensing education: Virginia requires aspiring brokers to complete 180 hours of approved real estate education. This includes 45 hours of Real Estate Brokerage Management, 45 hours of Real Estate Law, and 90 hours of other approved coursework.

3. Pass the state licensing exam: Once you have completed the required education, you must pass the Virginia real estate broker licensing exam. This exam covers both national and state-specific real estate laws and regulations.

4. Complete the application process: After passing the exam, you can submit your application for a real estate broker license to the Virginia Real Estate Board. The application includes a background check, fingerprinting, and a fee.

5. Obtain a sponsoring broker: As a new real estate broker in Virginia, you must work under the supervision of a licensed real estate broker. Find a sponsoring broker who will guide and mentor you as you begin your career.

6. Join a local association: Consider joining a local real estate association, such as the Virginia Association of Realtors. These associations provide valuable resources, networking opportunities, and professional development for real estate brokers.

7. Maintain your license: Once you have obtained your real estate broker license, it is essential to stay current with continuing education requirements and renew your license on time.

By following this step-by-step guide, you can successfully obtain your real estate broker license in Virginia. Remember to stay organized, stay informed, and take advantage of the resources available to you as you embark on your new career. Good luck!

Preparing for the Virginia Real Estate Broker Exam

Obtaining a real estate broker license in Virginia can be a profitable and fulfilling career move. However, before you can become a licensed broker in the state, you must successfully pass the Virginia Real Estate Broker Exam. This subchapter will guide you through the necessary steps to prepare for this exam and increase your chances of success.

1. Familiarize Yourself with Exam Format: The Virginia Real Estate Broker Exam consists of both national and state-specific questions. It assesses your knowledge of real estate principles, practices, and laws. Understanding the exam format and structure is crucial for effective preparation.

2. Study the Exam Content Outline: The Virginia Department of Professional and Occupational Regulation (DPOR) provides an exam content outline that details the topics and subtopics covered in the exam. This outline will serve as a roadmap for your study plan, ensuring you cover all the necessary areas.

3. Enroll in a Pre-Licensing Course: To meet the education requirement for the broker license, you must complete a DPOR-approved pre-licensing course. These courses cover essential topics such as agency relationships, contract law, finance, and property management. Attending a reputable course will provide you with comprehensive knowledge and help you prepare for the exam.

4. Utilize Study Materials: In addition to the pre-licensing course, you should supplement your studies with additional materials. Look for real estate exam prep books, online resources, and practice exams. These materials will give you a deeper understanding of the exam content and allow you to gauge your readiness.

5. Create a Study Schedule: A disciplined study schedule is crucial for effective preparation. Dedicate regular time slots to study and review

the exam content. Break down the topics into manageable sections and allocate sufficient time for each.

6. Take Practice Exams: Practice exams are a valuable tool for exam preparation. They simulate the actual exam experience, allowing you to identify areas of weakness and improve your test-taking skills. Work through a variety of practice exams to build confidence and familiarity with the exam format.

7. Seek Guidance and Support: Joining study groups and seeking guidance from experienced brokers can greatly enhance your preparation. Collaborating with others who are also preparing for the exam can provide different perspectives and insights. Additionally, consider reaching out to real estate professionals who have successfully passed the Virginia Real Estate Broker Exam for tips and advice.

By following these steps and putting in dedicated effort, you can effectively prepare for the Virginia Real Estate Broker Exam. Remember to stay focused, maintain a positive mindset, and utilize the available resources to maximize your chances of success. Good luck on your journey to becoming a licensed real estate broker in Virginia!

Important Considerations for Virginia License Applicants

Obtaining a real estate broker license in Virginia is an exciting endeavor that can open doors to a rewarding career in the real estate industry. However, it is crucial for license applicants to be aware of the important considerations specific to Virginia in order to navigate the application process successfully. This subchapter aims to provide real estate agents and the public with a comprehensive guide on the requirements and application process for a real estate broker license in Virginia.

One of the key considerations for Virginia license applicants is meeting the educational requirements. In Virginia, applicants must complete 180 hours of approved pre-licensing education, which typically covers topics such as real estate principles, practices, contracts, and laws. It is essential to choose an accredited education provider to ensure compliance with the state's requirements.

Another important consideration is passing the Virginia broker licensing exam. The exam evaluates applicants' knowledge and understanding of real estate principles and laws. It is crucial to thoroughly prepare for the exam by studying the recommended materials and taking practice tests. Additionally, applicants should be aware that the exam fee is non-refundable, so adequate preparation is essential to avoid unnecessary expenses.

In addition to the educational and exam requirements, Virginia license applicants must also submit an application to the Virginia Real Estate Board. The application process involves providing personal information, including a criminal background check, and paying the required fees. It is crucial to carefully complete the application and submit all necessary documents to avoid delays or rejection.

Furthermore, understanding the ongoing obligations and responsibilities of a licensed real estate broker in Virginia is vital. Licensees must comply with continuing education requirements to maintain their license. Virginia requires licensees to complete 24 hours of approved continuing education every two years, including three hours of ethics training. Staying informed about any updates or changes in the laws and regulations governing real estate in Virginia is also essential to ensure compliance.

By considering these important factors, real estate agents and the public can navigate the requirements and application process for a real estate broker license in Virginia more effectively. Obtaining a license in Virginia can be a significant step towards a successful and fulfilling career in the real estate industry.

# Chapter 11: Navigating the Real Estate Licensing Process in Washington, D.C.

Overview of the Washington, D.C. Real Estate Broker License Requirements

In the bustling city of Washington, D.C., the real estate market is thriving. Whether you are a real estate agent looking to take your career to the next level or a member of the public interested in understanding the requirements to become a licensed broker, this chapter will provide you with a step-by-step overview of the Washington, D.C. real estate broker license requirements.

To become a licensed real estate broker in Washington, D.C., there are a few key criteria that must be met. First and foremost, applicants must be at least 18 years old and have a high school diploma or equivalent. Additionally, they must have a minimum of three years of experience as a licensed real estate salesperson or broker.

Once these prerequisites are met, aspiring brokers must complete a 135-hour pre-licensing education program approved by the District of Columbia Real Estate Commission. This program covers various topics such as real estate law, finance, contracts, and ethics. It is crucial to choose a reputable education provider to ensure the program meets the commission's requirements.

After completing the pre-licensing education, applicants must pass the Washington, D.C. broker licensing exam. This exam tests their knowledge of real estate principles and practices, as well as their understanding of local laws and regulations. It is essential to study and prepare thoroughly to increase the chances of passing the exam on the first attempt.

Once the exam is successfully passed, applicants must submit their license application to the District of Columbia Real Estate Commission, along with the required documents and fees. These documents may include proof of education, experience, and a criminal background check.

It is important to note that maintaining a real estate broker license in Washington, D.C. requires continued education. Brokers must complete at least 15 hours of continuing education courses every two years to stay up-to-date with industry trends and regulations.

By understanding the Washington, D.C. real estate broker license requirements, both real estate agents and the public can navigate the licensing process with confidence. Whether you are looking to expand your career or simply want to gain a deeper understanding of the real estate industry, obtaining a broker license in Washington, D.C. can open doors to new opportunities and increased professional growth.

Step-by-Step Guide to Obtaining a Real Estate Broker License in Washington, D.C.

If you are a real estate agent or someone interested in pursuing a career in real estate brokerage in Washington, D.C., this step-by-step guide will provide you with all the information you need to obtain a real estate broker license in the District of Columbia.

Step 1: Meet the Basic Requirements

To qualify for a real estate broker license in Washington, D.C., you must be at least 18 years old, have a high school diploma or equivalent, and be of good character and reputation.

Step 2: Complete the Required Education

Washington, D.C. requires aspiring real estate brokers to complete 135 hours of pre-licensing education. This education must be obtained from an approved real estate school and covers various topics such as real estate law, finance, and contracts.

Step 3: Pass the Real Estate Broker Exam

After completing the required education, you must pass the real estate broker exam administered by the District of Columbia Real Estate Commission. This exam tests your knowledge of real estate principles and practices.

Step 4: Submit Your Application

Once you have passed the exam, you can submit your application for a real estate broker license. The application must include proof of completion of education, exam results, and a background check. You will also need to pay the required application fee.

Step 5: Obtain a Broker Sponsorship

To practice as a real estate broker in Washington, D.C., you must be sponsored by a licensed real estate broker. Find a broker who is willing to sponsor you and submit the necessary sponsorship forms to the Real Estate Commission.

Step 6: Complete the Post-Licensing Education

Within one year of obtaining your broker license, you must complete an additional 15 hours of post-licensing education. This education focuses on topics such as real estate ethics, fair housing, and agency relationships.

Step 7: Maintain Your Broker License

To maintain your real estate broker license in Washington, D.C., you must renew it every two years. This involves completing continuing education requirements and paying the renewal fee.

By following this step-by-step guide, you can navigate the process of obtaining a real estate broker license in Washington, D.C. Remember to stay updated on any changes to the licensing requirements and regulations to ensure your continued success in the real estate industry. Good luck on your journey to becoming a licensed real estate broker in the District of Columbia!

Preparing for the Washington, D.C. Real Estate Broker Exam

Before aspiring real estate agents can become licensed brokers in Washington, D.C., they must pass the Washington, D.C. Real Estate Broker Exam. This subchapter will provide valuable information and tips on how to prepare for this crucial exam.

The Washington, D.C. Real Estate Broker Exam is designed to assess the candidate's knowledge and understanding of real estate laws, regulations, and practices specific to the District of Columbia. To pass the exam, candidates must demonstrate proficiency in various areas, including real estate brokerage principles, contracts, finance, property management, and ethics.

To adequately prepare for the exam, aspiring brokers should consider taking a comprehensive pre-licensing course. These courses cover all the essential topics and provide in-depth instruction on the specific laws and regulations applicable to Washington, D.C. real estate. Many reputable real estate schools and online platforms offer such courses, which can greatly enhance the candidate's chances of passing the exam.

In addition to completing a pre-licensing course, candidates should also dedicate ample time to self-study and review. This involves thoroughly reading and understanding the Washington, D.C. Real Estate

Commission's Candidate Information Bulletin, which outlines the exam content and provides sample questions. By familiarizing themselves with the exam format and content, candidates can better focus their study efforts.

Practice exams are another valuable resource for exam preparation. These simulated exams provide candidates with an opportunity to assess their knowledge and identify areas that require further study. Many online platforms offer practice exams specifically tailored to the Washington, D.C. Real Estate Broker Exam, allowing candidates to gain confidence and improve their test-taking skills.

It is crucial for candidates to manage their time effectively during the exam. The Washington, D.C. Real Estate Broker Exam consists of a set number of multiple-choice questions, and candidates must complete the exam within the allotted time. Practicing under timed conditions can help candidates develop strategies for answering questions efficiently and avoiding time-consuming pitfalls.

In conclusion, preparing for the Washington, D.C. Real Estate Broker Exam requires a combination of comprehensive pre-licensing courses, self-study and review, practice exams, and effective time management. By investing time and effort into these preparations, aspiring real estate brokers can increase their chances of passing the exam and obtaining their license to practice in Washington, D.C.

Tips for a Smooth Licensing Process in Washington, D.C.

Obtaining a real estate broker license in Washington, D.C. can be a complex and time-consuming process. However, with the right knowledge and preparation, you can navigate the licensing process smoothly. This chapter will provide you with essential tips to ensure a successful licensing journey in Washington, D.C.

1. Understand the requirements: Before starting the licensing process, familiarize yourself with the specific requirements set by the District of Columbia Real Estate Commission (DCREC). These requirements include completing pre-licensing education, passing the licensing exam, and fulfilling any additional prerequisites.

2. Enroll in a reputable pre-licensing course: To meet the educational requirements, you must complete a specific number of hours of pre-licensing education from an approved provider. Research and enroll in a reputable course to ensure you receive the necessary knowledge and training.

3. Prepare for the licensing exam: The licensing exam is a crucial step in obtaining your broker license. Take advantage of exam preparation resources, such as practice exams and study guides, to familiarize yourself with the format and content. Dedicate sufficient time to study and review the relevant topics.

4. Gather required documentation: Washington, D.C. has specific documentation requirements that must be fulfilled when submitting your application. These may include proof of pre-licensing education, identification documents, and any other forms requested by the DCREC. Ensure you have all the necessary paperwork in order to prevent any delays in the licensing process.

5. Submit a complete application: Carefully review the application form and ensure that all sections are completed accurately. Incomplete or incorrect applications can lead to unnecessary delays or rejections. Double-check all information and attachments before submitting your application to the DCREC.

6. Allow ample time for processing: The licensing process in Washington, D.C. may take several weeks or even months. Plan accordingly and be patient during this waiting period. Avoid unnecessary

stress by submitting your application well in advance and following up with the DCREC if needed.

7. Stay informed: Keep yourself updated on any changes or updates to the licensing process in Washington, D.C. Visit the DCREC website regularly and sign up for email notifications to ensure you don't miss any important information.

By following these tips, you can streamline the process of obtaining a real estate broker license in Washington, D.C. Remember to stay organized, prepared, and proactive throughout the licensing journey. Good luck!